TEAM SPIRIT ®

SMART BOOKS FOR YOUNG FANS

THE CINCINNATI REDS

BY
MARK STEWART

NORWOODHOUSE PRESS

CHICAGO, ILLINOIS

Norwood House Press
P.O. Box 316598
Chicago, Illinois 60631

For information regarding Norwood House Press, please visit our website at:
www.norwoodhousepress.com or call 866-565-2900.

All photos courtesy of Getty Images except the following:
SportsChrome (4, 10, 11, 12, 14, 23, 35 bottom, 38), Author's Collection (6, 15, 24, 27, 33, 36, 43 top),
F.W. Rueckheim & Brother (7), Black Book Partners Archive (9, 37, 41), Gum, Inc. (17, 42 bottom),
TCMA, Ltd. (21), Topps, Inc. (22, 34 bottom right, 39, 40, 45), Wonder Books (28),
Fleer Corp. (30 both), Exhibit Supply Co. (34 bottom left), Goudey Gum Co. (42 top),
WKRC/Post Foods LLC (43 bottom), Matt Richman (48).
Cover Photo: Joe Robbins/Getty Images

The memorabilia and artifacts pictured in this book are presented for educational and informational purposes,
and come from the collection of the author.

Editor: Mike Kennedy
Designer: Ron Jaffe
Project Management: Black Book Partners, LLC.
Special thanks to Topps, Inc.

Library of Congress Cataloging-in-Publication Data

Stewart, Mark, 1960-
  The Cincinnati Reds / by Mark Stewart.
     p. cm. -- (Team spirit)
  Includes bibliographical references and index.
  Summary: "A Team Spirit Baseball edition featuring the Cincinnati Reds
that chronicles the history and accomplishments of the team. Includes access
to the Team Spirit website, which provides additional information, updates
and photos"--Provided by publisher.
  ISBN 978-1-59953-478-7 (library : alk. paper) -- ISBN 978-1-60357-358-0
(ebook) 1. Cincinnati Reds (Baseball team)--History--Juvenile literature.
I. Title.
  GV875.C65S837 2012
  796.357'640977178--dc23

                                                2011047943

Manufactured in the United States of America in North Mankato, Minnesota.
196N—012012

COVER PHOTO: The Reds celebrate a victory in 2011.

3 2530 60728 5788

TABLE OF CONTENTS

ABOUT OUR GLOSSARY

In this book, there may be several words that you are reading for the first time. Some are sports words, some are new vocabulary words, and some are familiar words that are used in an unusual way. All of these words are defined on page 46. Throughout the book, sports words appear in **bold type**. Regular vocabulary words appear in *bold italic type*.

MEET THE REDS

Once upon a time, every town in the country was a "baseball town." Over the years, other sports and teams competed with baseball for the attention of fans. But in Cincinnati, Ohio, baseball is still king. Every spring, the city buzzes with excitement as the Reds prepare for Opening Day. Every summer, the fans stream into the ballpark hoping their team will be playing for a championship that fall.

Players on the Reds are always excited to put on the team's uniform. They know that they will hear cheers for all their hard work. That's especially true when the Reds do the "little things" that fans in other cities might not even notice.

This book tells the story of the Reds. They look for players with modern skills who make an old-fashioned effort. The Reds are proud of their history, but they keep an eye on the future. In other words, the Reds make sure that baseball will always be Cincinnati's favorite game.

Brandon Phillips gets a warm welcome from teammates after scoring the winning run in a 2011 game.

In the years after the *Civil War*, baseball became a wildly popular sport in the United States. Everyone wanted to learn about the game, watch it, and play it. The best players were *professionals*.

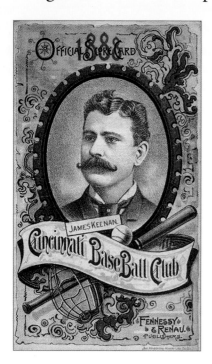

The first all-professional team took the field in Cincinnati in 1869. The club was called the Red Stockings. They weren't part of an organized league. Instead, the Red Stockings traveled from city to city to play any team that challenged them. Although that club went out of business, Cincinnati and its fans still see the city as the place where pro baseball got its start.

Today's Reds are connected to the Red Stockings in spirit, but the club actually dates back to 1882. That year, a new team called the Red Stockings began play in Cincinnati. That club was a member of a league known as the **American Association (AA)**. The stars of the Red Stockings were pitcher Will White and second baseman Bid McPhee. They led Cincinnati to its first AA championship. White was the first player to wear glasses on the field. McPhee was one of the last players to field without a mitt.

In 1890, the team joined the **National League (NL)** and changed its name to the Reds. Cincinnati won its first **pennant** in

GROH, Cincinnati Nationals

1919. That team was led by hitters Edd Roush, Heinie Groh, and Jake Daubert. The pitching staff featured Hod Eller, Slim Sallee, and Adolfo Luque. Luque was one of baseball's first Latino stars.

The Reds won the pennant again in 1939 and 1940. Those clubs had great pitching. Bucky Walters and Paul Derringer were two of the best starters in baseball. Ernie Lombardi and Frank McCormick provided power at the plate.

A *decade* later, the Reds developed into one of baseball's most dangerous offensive clubs. The Cincinnati teams of the 1950s were known for power hitters such as Frank Robinson, Gus Bell, Wally Post, and Ted Kluszewski. However, it was the scrappy and *tenacious* 1961 club that brought Cincinnati its

LEFT: A scorecard from an 1888 game shows Jim Keenan, the team's catcher.
ABOVE: Slugger Heinie Groh supplied the power for the 1919 Reds.

next pennant. Those Reds were a magical team—a different player seemed to make the winning play every day.

That was also the recipe for the success of the "Big Red Machine" of the 1970s. Pete Rose, Joe Morgan, Tony Perez, Johnny Bench, George Foster, and Ken Griffey Sr. formed the heart of a lineup that struck fear into opposing pitchers. Cincinnati won 90 or more games eight times during the decade. They also captured four pennants and two **World Series**.

The Reds won another championship in 1990. That team's hitting stars included Barry Larkin, Eric Davis, and Paul O'Neill. But Cincinnati won thanks to excellent pitching. The team's ace was Jose Rijo. The Reds also had a fearsome group of relief pitchers led by Rob Dibble, Norm Charlton, and Randy Myers. Together, they were known as the "Nasty Boys."

LEFT: Johnny Bench and Pete Rose were leaders of the "Big Red Machine" in the 1970s.   **ABOVE**: Barry Larkin

Larkin grew up in Cincinnati and ended up playing 19 years for the Reds. He led them to two first-place finishes during the 1990s and won the NL **Most Valuable Player (MVP)** award in 1995.

Despite their great success, the Reds often struggled to keep a winning team on the field as the 21st century opened. After moving into a new ballpark in 2003, the Reds began to rebuild around young players such as Joey Votto, Jay Bruce, Brandon Phillips, Drew Stubbs, Johnny Cueto, Yonder Alonso, and Aroldis Chapman. Before long, Cincinnati was again in position to compete for a championship.

In 2010, the Reds made it back to the **playoffs** for the first time since 1995. They clinched the **NL Central** crown in a thrilling

game against the Houston Astros. Stubbs reached over the fence to prevent a two-run homer, and Bruce won the game in the bottom of the 9th inning with a home run. It was only the fifth time in history that a **walk-off** homer sent a team to the playoffs.

After the season, Votto was named MVP of the league. Meanwhile, more top talent kept flowing into the Cincinnati lineup, including pitchers Mat Latos and Sean Marshall. By 2012, the Reds had one of the youngest, most exciting teams in baseball. Their third century of baseball was already looking as good as their first two.

LEFT: Jay Bruce   **ABOVE**: Joey Votto

HOME TURF

From 1912 to 1970, the Reds played in Crosley Field. It was one of the first modern stadiums in the **big leagues**. In 1935, Crosley Field was the first to install lights for night baseball. Midway through 1970, the Reds moved to Riverfront Stadium. It was one of the first ballparks to have *artificial turf*.

In 2003, the Reds opened a new stadium called Great American Ball Park. It's a modern stadium with an old-time feel. Fans enter through Crosley Terrace, an area that brings back memories of Crosley Field. Once inside, they see fun, exciting baseball. When a Cincinnati player launches a home run, fireworks shoot out from two 64-foot smokestacks behind the right field wall.

BY THE NUMBERS

- The Reds' stadium has 42,271 seats.
- The distance from home plate to the left field foul pole is 328 feet.
- The distance from home plate to the center field fence is 404 feet.
- The distance from home plate to the right field foul pole is 325 feet.

Hitters like the Reds' stadium because it's not hard to clear the fences for a home run.

DRESSED FOR SUCCESS

The Reds were once baseball's most colorful team. In their first season, each player wore a different colored silk uniform and cap. Since then, the main uniform color has been—what else?—red.

During their early years, the Reds wore bright white uniforms at home and dark blue uniforms on the road. In the years since, the team has mostly featured red and white, though black has also become a team color. During the 1950s and 1960s, the Reds used sleeveless jerseys. The team brings back the sleeveless jerseys for special occasions. The Reds' *logo* is a *C* with the team name inside.

During the 1950s, Cincinnati changed its team name temporarily to "Redlegs." Why the different name? After *World War II*, "Reds" was a term used for enemies of the United States. During that time, the team switched its logo to a baseball-shaped man with an old-time cap and moustache.

LEFT: Aroldis Chapman wears the team's home uniform during a 2011 game.
ABOVE: Leo Cardenas wears the Reds' sleeveless jersey.

WE WON!

In 1882, Cincinnati's Red Stockings won the American Association championship. To determine the champion of all of baseball, they played the Chicago White Stockings, the NL pennant winner. The

series was stopped after the teams split the first two games. The AA did not want the rival leagues to mix. Still, this is considered by many fans to be the first World Series.

The Reds won their next pennant in 1919. The team had only one big star—batting champion Edd Roush—but it had a brilliant manager named Pat Moran. He guided Cincinnati to victory over the mighty Chicago White Sox in the World Series. Afterward,

LEFT: Reds manager Pat Moran shakes hands with Chicago's Kid Gleason before the 1919 World Series.
RIGHT: Paul Derringer beat the Detroit Tigers twice in the 1940 World Series, including Game 7.

it was discovered that gamblers had tried to pay players on both sides to make bad plays. None of the Reds had accepted this offer, but some of the White Sox had. Those players were thrown out of baseball.

During the 1930s, the Reds built a very good club. Pitchers Bucky Walters, Paul Derringer, and Johnny Vander Meer led the team on the mound. Catcher Ernie Lombardi, first baseman Frank McCormick, and outfielder Ival Goodman supplied the hitting. The Reds won the pennant in 1939 and 1940. The 1940 team defeated the Detroit Tigers in the World Series.

The Reds had their ups and downs over the next 30 years. Their one great season during that period came in 1961. Joey Jay, the first Little Leaguer to play in the majors, joined the club and won 21 games. Frank Robinson and Vada Pinson had amazing years at the plate. Those three stars led a ragtag club to the pennant.

The Reds rebuilt their team during the 1960s, and by the 1970s they had become the Big Red Machine. Cincinnati won games with **All-Star** hitters Johnny Bench, Pete Rose, Joe Morgan, Tony Perez, and Ken Griffey Sr. They also had great pitching when it counted most—at the end of games. Manager Sparky Anderson built a deep and talented **bullpen** that included Clay Carroll, Pedro Borbon, and Rawly Eastwick.

The Reds captured the pennant four times from 1970 to 1976. In 1975, they faced the Boston Red Sox in the World Series. Cincinnati won three games in its last turn at bat, including Game 7. The Reds were crowned champions of baseball for the third time. The following year, Cincinnati swept the New York Yankees in four games to repeat as champions. Rose, Morgan, and Bench were the big heroes.

Cincinnati's most remarkable championship came in 1990. That team was led by three overpowering relief pitchers—Rob Dibble, Randy Myers, and Norm Charlton. The Reds played the Oakland A's in the World Series. Some fans wondered if Cincinnati would win a single game. Instead, the Reds won four straight against Oakland. Pitcher Jose Rijo and hitters Chris Sabo and Billy Hatcher were the stars in the team's fifth and final championship of the 20th century.

LEFT: Joe Morgan rounds third base during the 1976 World Series.   **RIGHT**: The Reds race onto the field after winning the 1990 World Series.

GO-TO GUYS

To be a true star in baseball, you need more than a quick bat and a strong arm. You have to be a "go-to guy"—someone the manager wants on the pitcher's mound or in the batter's box when it matters most. Fans of the Reds have had a lot to cheer about over the years, including these great stars …

THE PIONEERS

BID McPHEE   Second Baseman

- BORN: 11/1/1859   • DIED: 1/3/1943   • PLAYED FOR TEAM: 1882 TO 1899

Bid McPhee was known for his sportsmanship during a time when baseball could be a dirty game. He was a good hitter and a great defensive player. McPhee fielded bare-handed long after other players started wearing gloves. He entered the **Hall of Fame** in 2009.

EDD ROUSH   Outfielder

- BORN: 5/8/1893   • DIED: 3/21/1988   • PLAYED FOR TEAM: 1916 TO 1926 & 1931

Edd Roush was the best center fielder in the NL when he played for the Reds. He won batting championships in 1917 and 1919. Roush used a thick-handled bat that weighed much more than bats used today.

ERNIE LOMBARDI   Catcher

- BORN: 4/6/1908 • DIED: 9/26/1977 • PLAYED FOR TEAM: 1932 TO 1941

Ernie Lombardi had a quick bat and slow feet. He batted .300 seven times but was thrown out at first base several times on balls to right field that seemed like sure hits. Lombardi won the league MVP in 1938.

TED KLUSZEWSKI   First Baseman

- BORN: 9/10/1924 • DIED: 3/29/1988
- PLAYED FOR TEAM: 1947 TO 1957

Ted Kluszewski's arms were so thick that he had to cut the sleeves off his uniform to swing. In 1954, "Big Klu" led the NL in home runs and **runs batted in (RBIs)**. In 1955, he hit 47 homers and struck out only 47 times.

FRANK ROBINSON   Outfielder

- BORN: 8/31/1935 • PLAYED FOR TEAM: 1956 TO 1965

Frank Robinson played as hard as anyone who ever wore a Cincinnati uniform. He was a dangerous hitter, a daring baserunner, and a good fielder. Robinson was named NL MVP in 1961, when he led Cincinnati to the World Series.

ABOVE: Ted Kluszewski

PETE ROSE   Infielder/Outfielder

• BORN: 4/14/1941   • PLAYED FOR TEAM: 1963 TO 1978 & 1984 TO 1986

Pete Rose loved to play baseball. He hustled on every play and even ran to first base after being walked. Rose won three batting titles with the Reds and played 500 games at five different positions. When he retired, he had 4,256 hits, more than anyone in history.

JOHNNY BENCH   Catcher

• BORN: 12/7/1947   • PLAYED FOR TEAM: 1967 TO 1983

No other catcher in the 1970s compared to Johnny Bench. He had the strongest arm and most powerful bat of anyone at his position. Bench won two MVP awards and 10 **Gold Gloves**. Many believe he was the greatest catcher in baseball history.

JOE MORGAN   Second Baseman

• BORN: 9/19/1943

• PLAYED FOR TEAM: 1972 TO 1979

Joe Morgan was a run-scoring machine. He was a smart, patient hitter and a very good base-stealer. In 1975 and 1976, Morgan was the league MVP. It was just the second time in history that an NL player earned the award two years in a row.

BARRY LARKIN   Shortstop

- BORN: 4/28/1964   • PLAYED FOR TEAM: 1986 TO 2004

Barry Larkin was born and raised in Cincinnati. He was a star in his hometown for nearly 20 seasons. Larkin won the MVP award in 1995. The following year, he became the first shortstop to hit 30 homers and steal 30 bases in the same season.

JOEY VOTTO   First Baseman

- BORN: 9/10/1983   • FIRST YEAR WITH TEAM: 2007

In 2008, Joey Votto broke Frank Robinson's team record for RBIs by a **rookie**. Two years later, Votto had an even better season and was named MVP. He was just the third Canadian-born player to win the award.

JOHNNY CUETO   Pitcher

- BORN: 2/15/1986   • FIRST YEAR WITH TEAM: 2008

Johnny Cueto struck out 10 batters in his first game for the Reds. It had been more than 100 years since a Cincinnati pitcher had done that. In 2011, his 2.31 **earned run average (ERA)** was one of the lowest for a starter in the big leagues.

LEFT: Joe Morgan
RIGHT: Johnny Cueto

T he first great leader in Reds' history was Garry Herrmann. He was one of the most powerful people in baseball in the early 1900s while he was the club's president. In the 1930s, Powel Crosley bought the team. He had a knack for hiring brilliant **executives**, including Larry MacPhail, Warren Giles, Frank Lane, and Gabe Paul. All would become baseball legends.

Cincinnati has also had many excellent managers over the years, including Pat Moran, Bill McKechnie, and Fred Hutchinson. Each led the Reds to the top of the league. The team's most famous manager was Sparky Anderson, who walked the dugout from 1970 to 1978. Anderson stressed the basics. He was a good teacher of young players and placed great responsibility on the shoulders of his older players.

Anderson put the most pressure on his pitchers. He expected them to make every pitch a good one. If Anderson believed a

starting pitcher was tired, injured, or just losing his focus, he would bounce out of the dugout and take the ball away. Then it would be up to the next pitcher to finish the job. Fans joked that Anderson was quick to give his pitchers the hook. This was an old show-business saying. Soon, Anderson was known as "Captain Hook."

Anderson understood the importance of relief pitchers and used them more effectively than any other manager of his time. He set the standard for every manager that followed him in Cincinnati. The Reds had plenty of good ones, including Pete Rose, Lou Piniella, and Davey Johnson. All relied on timely hitting and strong pitching—the same formula that made Anderson so successful.

LEFT: Garry Herrmann   **ABOVE**: Sparky Anderson

ONE GREAT DAY

Hard as it may be to imagine, there once was a time when every baseball game was played during the day. That meant that children could usually only go to games on the weekend or while on summer vacation. Adults had to leave their jobs early to see games played Monday through Friday. And when darkness fell, the umpires stopped the game. This was because big-league stadiums did not have lights for evening baseball.

That changed on a spring night in 1935. The Reds began their game against the Philadelphia Phillies as the sun was setting. But the players and fans were able to see the ball thanks to 632 lights that had been installed on the roof of Crosley Field. Each bulb was 1,500 watts—more than 20 times more powerful than the ones people used in homes. Though these lights were not as powerful as those in today's stadiums, the players said they could see as well as they did on a cloudy day.

This souvenir postcard shows baseball "under the lights" in Cincinnati.

More than 20,000 fans watched the Reds battle the Phillies. Paul Derringer pitched all nine innings for Cincinnati in a 2–1 victory. He allowed just six hits and did not walk a batter. Billy Sullivan, the Reds' first baseman, led both teams with two hits. Afterwards he joked, "There was electricity in the air!"

Night baseball had been tried before, in the **minor leagues**. The lighting was not powerful enough, however. Many times the outfielders could barely be seen from home plate. Batters complained that half the ball was in shadows. Thanks to the powerful lights in Cincinnati, there were no such complaints.

The Reds' success convinced other teams to play at night. Although it was more expensive to host evening games—because of the electric bills—teams still made lots of money from these contests. Thousands of fans who could not see weekday baseball because of jobs and school were now able to attend games. Today, teams typically play more than half their games after sundown.

LEGEND HAS IT

WHO WAS THE REDS' BEST FOOTBALL PLAYER?

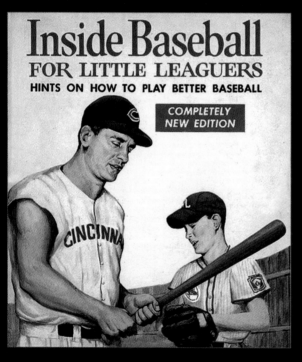

LEGEND HAS IT that Ted Kluszewski was. Kluszewski was a football star for Indiana University during the 1940s. In the spring of 1945, the Reds held training camp on the school's campus. After the team left for the locker room one day, a groundskeeper noticed a student whacking balls over an embankment in the outfield. None of the Cincinnati hitters had been able to reach the little hill during batting practice. The hitter was Kluszewski. The Reds made sure they signed him after he graduated in 1946.

ABOVE: This 1950s children's book shows Ted Kluszewski's rock-solid "football" body.

WHICH RED ONCE OUTRAN A CHEETAH?

LEGEND HAS IT that Billy Bates did. Bates was a member of the Reds in the 1990s. As a young player trying to impress his teammates, he agreed to run against a cheetah from the Cincinnati Zoo in a 100-yard race. Bates was given a five-second head start. His cap flew off as he sprinted from the starting line. The cheetah immediately pounced on the bright red cap. Bates looked back and began to worry that he might be next on the menu. He ran even faster and crossed the finish line first.

WHICH PLAYER HAD THE BEST START EVER TO A WORLD SERIES?

LEGEND HAS IT that Billy Hatcher did. Hatcher played left field and batted .276 for the Reds when they won the NL pennant in 1990. As the Oakland A's prepared to meet Cincinnati in the World Series, they were more worried about Barry Larkin, Eric Davis, and Paul O'Neill. However, it was Hatcher who became the hitting star. In Game 1, he reached base on a walk and had a single and two doubles. In Game 2, he had a single, two doubles, a triple, and another walk. The A's did not get him out until Game 3, and he still got two hits in that game!

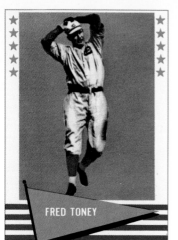

FRED TONEY

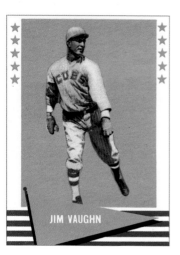

JIM VAUGHN

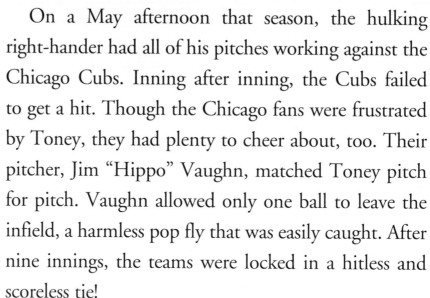

The Reds were a team on the rise in 1917. One very big reason was pitcher Fred Toney. At the time, he was known as one of the biggest and strongest players in history.

On a May afternoon that season, the hulking right-hander had all of his pitches working against the Chicago Cubs. Inning after inning, the Cubs failed to get a hit. Though the Chicago fans were frustrated by Toney, they had plenty to cheer about, too. Their pitcher, Jim "Hippo" Vaughn, matched Toney pitch for pitch. Vaughn allowed only one ball to leave the infield, a harmless pop fly that was easily caught. After nine innings, the teams were locked in a hitless and scoreless tie!

The Reds came to bat in the top of the 10th inning. With one out, Larry Kopf slashed a single to right field for the first hit of the game. Next, Hal Chase hit a line drive that was dropped, and Kopf raced to third base. Jim Thorpe was the next batter. He was a famous

football star who played outfield for the Reds. Thorpe took a mighty swing but rolled a weak grounder to Vaughn, who bounded off the pitcher's mound to field the ball. He threw to the catcher, but Kopf slid home safely as the ball bounced away.

Toney took the mound one more time and retired all three Chicago batters to give the Reds a 1–0 victory. It was the first (and last) time in history that two teams played nine innings without getting a hit.

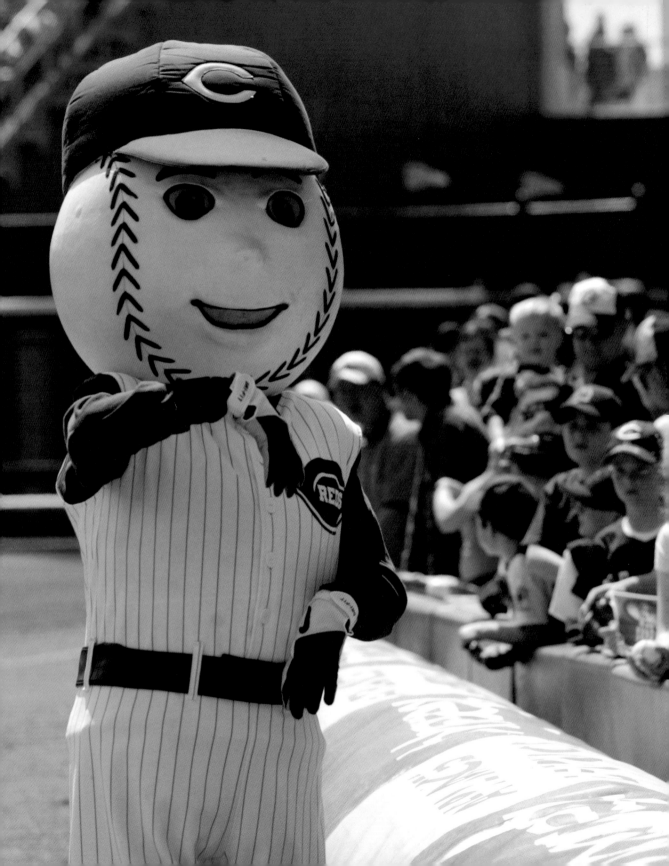

TEAM SPIRIT

Cincinnati was home to America's first professional baseball team in 1869. The people of the city have been baseball-crazy ever since. Their bond with the Reds goes back more than a century. For many decades, the Reds had the honor of playing the first game of the season.

Cincinnati fans were the first in the major leagues to watch night baseball. They were also the first to "stuff" the ballot box for the **All-Star Game**. In 1957, they voted so often for their favorite players that seven of the eight starting fielders for the NL were Reds!

The team's new ballpark is a great *thank you* to fans for years of loyalty. Beyond the outfield wall is the Fan Zone. It has a great view of the field and the Ohio River. It also has interactive games and live music. Mr. Red and Gapper—the team's two mascots—usually start games at the Fan Zone and then roam throughout the ballpark.

LEFT: Mr. Red greets the Cincinnati crowd.
ABOVE: This button was worn by Reds fans during the 1950s.

TIMELINE

Joe DiMaggio and Frank McCormick meet before the 1939 World Series.

1890
The Reds join the National League.

1940
Frank McCormick leads the NL in hits for the third year in a row.

1882
The Reds play their first season and win the AA championship.

1919
The Reds win their first World Series.

1956
Frank Robinson is named **Rookie of the Year**.

Ivey Wingo batted .571 in the 1919 World Series.

Frank Robinson

FRANK ROBINSON   of

Pete Rose meets Tommy Holmes, the player whose record he broke.

1978
Pete Rose sets an NL record with a 44-game hitting streak.

1990
The Reds sweep the Oakland A's in the World Series.

2010
Joey Votto is named MVP.

1976
The Reds win their second World Series in a row.

1995
Barry Larkin is named MVP.

2004
Ken Griffey Jr. hits his 500th home run.

"Junior" watches a home run leave the park.

Fun Facts

Twice as Nice

In 1938, Johnny Vander Meer pitched a **no-hitter** against the Boston Bees. Four days later, he pitched against the Dodgers in Brooklyn and no-hit them, too. No pitcher before or since has pitched two no-hitters in a row.

Double the Fun

In 2009, Joey Votto hit 10 doubles during a five-day period. It was the first time a player had done this since 1932.

First in Flight

From 1911 to 1914, Armando Marsans of Cuba played outfield for the Reds. He was a great fielder and one of the fastest, most daring runners in the league, too. Marsans was the first Spanish-speaking player to be a star in the major leagues.

ALMOST PERFECT

Bret Boone was the league's best-fielding second baseman three years in a row with the Reds. In 1997, his **fielding average** was .997—the highest in history for a player at that position.

HOME RUN HAPPY

In 1999, the Reds hit nine home runs in a game against the Philadelphia Phillies. That broke the NL record of eight, which was first set by the Reds in 1956.

THE OL' LEFT-HANDER

During World War II, the Reds were desperate for pitching. In 1944, they sent 15-year-old Joe Nuxhall to the mound. He was the youngest player in baseball history. Nuxhall went on to win 136 games for the Reds and later announced their games on radio and television. After every game, he would sign off by saying, "This is the ol' left-hander, rounding third and heading for home."

LEFT: Johnny Vander Meer signed this photo with the dates of his no-hitters.
ABOVE: Bret Boone led the NL in fielding from 1995 to 1997.

TALKING BASEBALL

"I'm strictly concerned about winning and getting into the playoffs."

▶ **JOEY VOTTO**, ON WHY HE PLAYS THE GAME

"Every time I put on this uniform, I felt like I'm living a dream."

▶ **SEAN CASEY**, ON THE THRILL OF PLAYING FOR THE REDS

"I always tried to do the best. I knew I couldn't always be the best, but I tried to be."

▶ **FRANK ROBINSON**, ON GIVING 100 PERCENT WHENEVER HE TOOK THE FIELD

"Pete Rose is Cincinnati. He's the Reds."

▶ **SPARKY ANDERSON**, ON THE PLAYER THAT MANY FANS CONSIDER THE BEST IN TEAM HISTORY

"If you want to be a catcher, watch Johnny Bench."

▶ *PETE ROSE, ON THE BEST WAY TO LEARN HOW TO PLAY BEHIND THE PLATE*

"I take my vote as a salute to the little guy, the one who doesn't hit 500 home runs. I was one of the guys that did all they could to win."

▶ *JOE MORGAN, ON BEING VOTED INTO THE HALL OF FAME*

"I can throw out any man alive."

▶ *JOHNNY BENCH, ON THE STRENGTH OF HIS ARM*

"Those people that were at Crosley Field that afternoon probably said, 'Well, that's the last we'll see of that kid.'"

▶ *JOE NUXHALL, ON JOINING THE REDS AS A TEENAGER IN 1944 ... AND THEN STAYING WITH THE TEAM FOR MORE THAN 50 YEARS*

LEFT: Joey Votto   **ABOVE**: Johnny Bench

GREAT DEBATES

People who root for the Reds love to compare their favorite moments, teams, and players. Some debates have been going on for years! How would you settle these classic baseball arguments?

PETE ROSE'S RECORD-BREAKING HIT IN 1985 WAS THE BEST MOMENT IN REDS HISTORY ...

... because he passed one of baseball's greatest players, Ty Cobb. Rose (   ) smacked a single against the San Diego Padres to become the sport's all-time leader in hits. Most experts thought Cobb would hold this record forever. It took Rose 23 seasons to break it. During that time, he was an All-Star 17 times and won three batting championships.

DON'T TELL THAT TO JOHNNY VANDER MEER FANS ...

... because they are still waiting for someone to pitch back-to-back no-hitters. Vander Meer blanked the Boston Braves in Cincinnati on June 11, 1938. Then he did the same to the Brooklyn Dodgers four days later. Vander Meer was pitching in his first full season. He went on to win 119 games for the Reds. Will anyone break his record? They would have to pitch three no-hitters in a row. So the answer is almost certainly *NO!*

... because they were simply unstoppable. Imagine standing on the pitcher's mound having to face one Hall of Famer after another. Johnny Bench, Pete Rose, Tony Perez, and Joe Morgan gave the Big Red Machine an overpowering batting order. Even if you got those guys out, you still had to deal with George Foster, Ken Griffey Sr., and Dave Concepcion. Foster hit 52 homers one year. Concepcion was a great clutch hitter. And Griffey hit better than .300 six times.

THERE WAS NOTHING MIRACULOUS ABOUT THE 1990 REDS ...

... because they won by playing good baseball. Cincinnati had players such as Paul O'Neill (   ) who were smart hitters, excellent fielders, and daring baserunners. The team had strong starting pitchers and great relievers, too. In fact, it would be fun to see the Big Red Machine try to get a hit off of the Nasty Boys. Norm Charlton, Rob Dibble, and Randy Myers were three of the scariest relief pitchers who ever played the game.

FOR THE RECORD

T he great Reds teams and players have left their marks on the record books. These are the "best of the best" ...

Ernie Lombardi

"BUCKY" WALTERS

Bucky Walters

REDS AWARD WINNERS

WINNER	AWARD	YEAR
Ernie Lombardi	Most Valuable Player	1938
Bucky Walters	Most Valuable Player	1939
Frank McCormick	Most Valuable Player	1940
Frank Robinson	Rookie of the Year	1956
Frank Robinson	Most Valuable Player	1961
Pete Rose	Rookie of the Year	1963
Tommy Helms	Rookie of the Year	1966
Tony Perez	All-Star Game MVP	1967
Johnny Bench	Rookie of the Year	1968
Johnny Bench	Most Valuable Player	1970
Joe Morgan	All-Star Game MVP	1972
Johnny Bench	Most Valuable Player	1972
Pete Rose	Most Valuable Player	1973
Joe Morgan	Most Valuable Player	1975
Pete Rose	World Series MVP	1975
George Foster	All-Star Game MVP	1976
Joe Morgan	Most Valuable Player	1976
Pat Zachry	Rookie of the Year	1976
Johnny Bench	World Series MVP	1976
George Foster	Most Valuable Player	1977
Ken Griffey Sr.	All-Star Game MVP	1980
Dave Concepcion	All-Star Game MVP	1982
Chris Sabo	Rookie of the Year	1988
Jose Rijo	World Series MVP	1990
Barry Larkin	Most Valuable Player	1995
Scott Williamson	Rookie of the Year	1999
Jack McKeon	Manager of the Year	1999
Joey Votto	Most Valuable Player	2010

ACHIEVEMENT	YEAR
AA Champions	1882
NL pennant Winners	1919
World Series Champions	1919
NL Pennant Winners	1939
NL Pennant Winners	1940
World Series Champions	1940
NL Pennant Winners	1961
NL West Champions	1970
NL Pennant Winners	1970
NL West Champions	1972
NL Pennant Winners	1972
NL West Champions	1973
NL West Champions	1975
NL Pennant Winners	1975
World Series Champions	1975
NL West Champions	1976
NL Pennant Winners	1976
World Series Champions	1976
NL West Champions	1979
NL West Champions	1990
NL Pennant Winners	1990
World Series Champions	1990
NL Central Champions	1994
NL Central Champions	1995
NL Central Champions	2010

ABOVE: Frank Robinson takes a swing. He was the NL's top rookie in 1956.
LEFT: Johnny Vander Meer and Frank McCormick led the Reds to the pennant in 1939 and 1940.

PINPOINTS

The history of a baseball team is made up of many smaller stories. These stories take place all over the map—not just in the city a team calls "home." Match the pushpins on these maps to the **TEAM FACTS**, and you will begin to see the story of the Reds unfold!

1 Cincinnati, Ohio—*The Reds have played here since 1882.*

2 Boston, Massachusetts—*The Reds won the 1975 World Series here.*

3 Oakland, California—*The Reds played in the 1972 World Series here.*

4 Beaumont, Texas—*Frank Robinson was born here.*

5 New York, New York—*The Reds won the 1976 World Series here.*

6 Bridgewater, South Dakota—*Sparky Anderson was born here.*

7 Argo, Illinois—*Ted Kluszewski was born here.*

8 Tuscaloosa, Alabama—*George Foster was born here.*

9 Los Angeles, California—*Eric Davis was born here.*

10 San Cristobal, Dominican Republic—*Jose Rijo was born here.*

11 Ocumare de la Costa, Venezuela—*Dave Concepcion was born here.*

12 Havana, Cuba—*Adolfo Luque was born here.*

Dave Concepcion

GLOSSARY

🗣 **ALL-STAR**—Selected to play in baseball's annual All-Star Game.

🗣 **ALL-STAR GAME**—Baseball's annual game featuring the best players from the American League and National League.

🗣 **AMERICAN ASSOCIATION (AA)**—A rival to the National League in the 1800s. The AA played from 1882 to 1891.

🧠 *ARTIFICIAL TURF*—A playing surface made from fake grass.

🗣 **BIG LEAGUES**—The top level of professional baseball; also known as the majors.

🗣 **BULLPEN**—The area where a team's relief pitchers warm up. This word also describes the group of relief pitchers in this area.

🧠 *CIVIL WAR*—The American war fought between armies of the North and South from 1861 to 1865.

🧠 *DECADE*—A period of 10 years; also specific periods, such as the 1950.

🗣 **EARNED RUN AVERAGE (ERA)**—A statistic that measures how many runs a pitcher gives up for every nine innings he pitches.

🧠 *EXECUTIVES*—People who make important decisions for a company.

🗣 **FIELDING AVERAGE**—A statistic that measures a player's defensive ability.

🗣 **GOLD GLOVES**—The awards given each year to baseball's best fielders.

🗣 **HALL OF FAME**—The museum in Cooperstown, New York, where baseball's greatest players are honored. A player voted into the Hall of Fame is sometimes called a "Hall of Famer."

🧠 *LOGO*—A symbol or design that represents a company or team.

🗣 **MINOR LEAGUES**—The many professional leagues that help develop players for the major leagues.

🗣 **MOST VALUABLE PLAYER (MVP)**—The award given each year to each league's top player; an MVP is also selected for the World Series and the All-Star Game.

🗣 **NATIONAL LEAGUE (NL)**—The older of the two major leagues; the NL began play in 1876.

🗣 **NL CENTRAL**—A group of National League teams that play in the central part of the country.

🗣 **NO-HITTER**—A game in which a team does not get a hit.

🗣 **PENNANT**—A league championship. The term comes from the triangular flag awarded to each season's champion, beginning in the 1870s.

🗣 **PLAYOFFS**—The games played after the regular season to determine which teams will advance to the World Series.

🧠 *PROFESSIONALS*—People who are paid to do a job.

🗣 **ROOKIE**—A player in his first season.

🗣 **ROOKIE OF THE YEAR**—The annual award given to each league's best first-year player.

🗣 **RUNS BATTED IN (RBIs)**—A statistic that counts the number of runners a batter drives home.

🧠 *TENACIOUS*—Refusing to give up.

🗣 **WALK-OFF**—Game-ending. After a walk-off hit, the teams simply walk off the field.

🗣 **WORLD SERIES**—The world championship series played between the American League and National League pennant winners.

🧠 *WORLD WAR II*—The war between the major powers of Europe, Asia, and North America that lasted from 1939 to 1945. The United States entered the war in 1941.

EXTRA INNINGS

TEAM SPIRIT introduces a great way to stay up to date with your team! Visit our **EXTRA INNINGS** link and get connected to the latest and greatest updates. **EXTRA INNINGS** serves as a young reader's ticket to an exclusive web page—with more stories, fun facts, team records, and photos of the Reds. Content is updated during and after each season. The **EXTRA INNINGS** feature also enables readers to send comments and letters to the author! Log onto:

www.norwoodhousepress.com/library.aspx

and click on the tab: **TEAM SPIRIT** to access **EXTRA INNINGS**.

Read all the books in the series to learn more about professional sports. For a complete listing of the baseball, basketball, football, and hockey teams in the **TEAM SPIRIT** series, visit our website at:

www.norwoodhousepress.com/library.aspx

ON THE ROAD

CINCINNATI REDS
100 Main Street
Cincinnati, Ohio 45202
(513) 765-7000
cincinnati.reds.mlb.com

**NATIONAL BASEBALL
HALL OF FAME AND MUSEUM**
25 Main Street
Cooperstown, New York 13326
(888) 425-5633
www.baseballhalloffame.org

ON THE BOOKSHELF

To learn more about the sport of baseball, look for these books at your library or bookstore:

- Augustyn, Adam (editor). *The Britannica Guide to Baseball*. New York, NY: Rosen Publishing, 2011.

- Dreier, David. *Baseball: How It Works*. North Mankato, MN: Capstone Press, 2010.

- Stewart, Mark. *Ultimate 10: Baseball*. New York, NY: Gareth Stevens Publishing, 2009.

INDEX

ABOUT THE AUTHOR

MARK STEWART has written more than 50 books on baseball and over 150 sports books for kids. He grew up in New York City during the 1960s rooting for the Yankees and Mets, and was lucky enough to meet players from both teams. Mark comes from a family of writers. His grandfather was Sunday Editor of *The New York Times,* and his mother was Articles Editor of *Ladies' Home Journal* and *McCall's.* Mark has profiled hundreds of athletes over the past 25 years. He has also written several books about his native New York and New Jersey, his home today. Mark is a graduate of Duke University, with a degree in history. He lives and works in a home overlooking Sandy Hook, New Jersey. You can contact Mark through the Norwood House Press website.